WHAT'S INSIDE A Digital Camera?

ARNOLD RINGSTAD

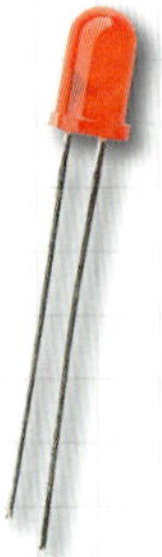

Published by The Child's World®
1980 Lookout Drive • Mankato, MN 56003-1705
800-599-READ • www.childsworld.com

Photographs ©: Rick Orndorf, cover (camera), 1 (camera), 4, 7, 8, 9, 11 (top), 11 (bottom), 13, 15, 16 (bottom), 17 (top left), 17 (top right), 19, 20 (lens), 24; Shutterstock Images, cover (screw), 1 (screw), 2, 3 (plug), 3 (circuit board), 5 (glasses), 6 (screw), 10 (circuit board), 12 (screw), 14, 16 (top), 20 (circuit board), 22; Jiradet Ponari/Shutterstock Images, cover (memory card), 1 (memory card), 6 (memory card), 12 (memory card), 17 (bottom), 18 (memory card); Praiwun Thungsarn/Shutterstock Images, 3 (screwdriver), 5 (screwdriver), 18 (screwdriver); Shyripa Alexandr/Shutterstock Images, 5 (gloves); Oleksandr Kostiuchenko/Shutterstock Images, 10 (battery), 23

ISBN 9781503832381
LCCN 2018963101

Printed in the United States of America
PA02419

About the Author

Arnold Ringstad lives in Minnesota. He takes pictures with digital cameras all the time.

Contents

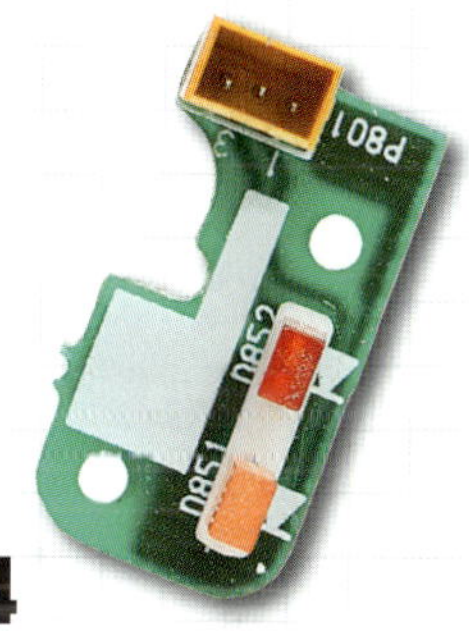

Materials and Safety

Materials

- ☐ Digital camera
- ☐ Phillips screwdriver
- ☐ Safety glasses
- ☐ Work gloves

Safety

- Be careful when handling sharp objects, such as screwdrivers.
- Wear work gloves to protect your hands from sharp edges.
- Wear safety glasses in case pieces snap off.

Digital camera

Important!

Be sure to get an adult's permission before taking anything apart. When you're taking things apart, have an adult nearby in case you need help or have questions.

Inside a Digital Camera

Digital cameras make taking pictures easy. These cameras are small and light. They can store hundreds of pictures. How do digital cameras work? What's inside?

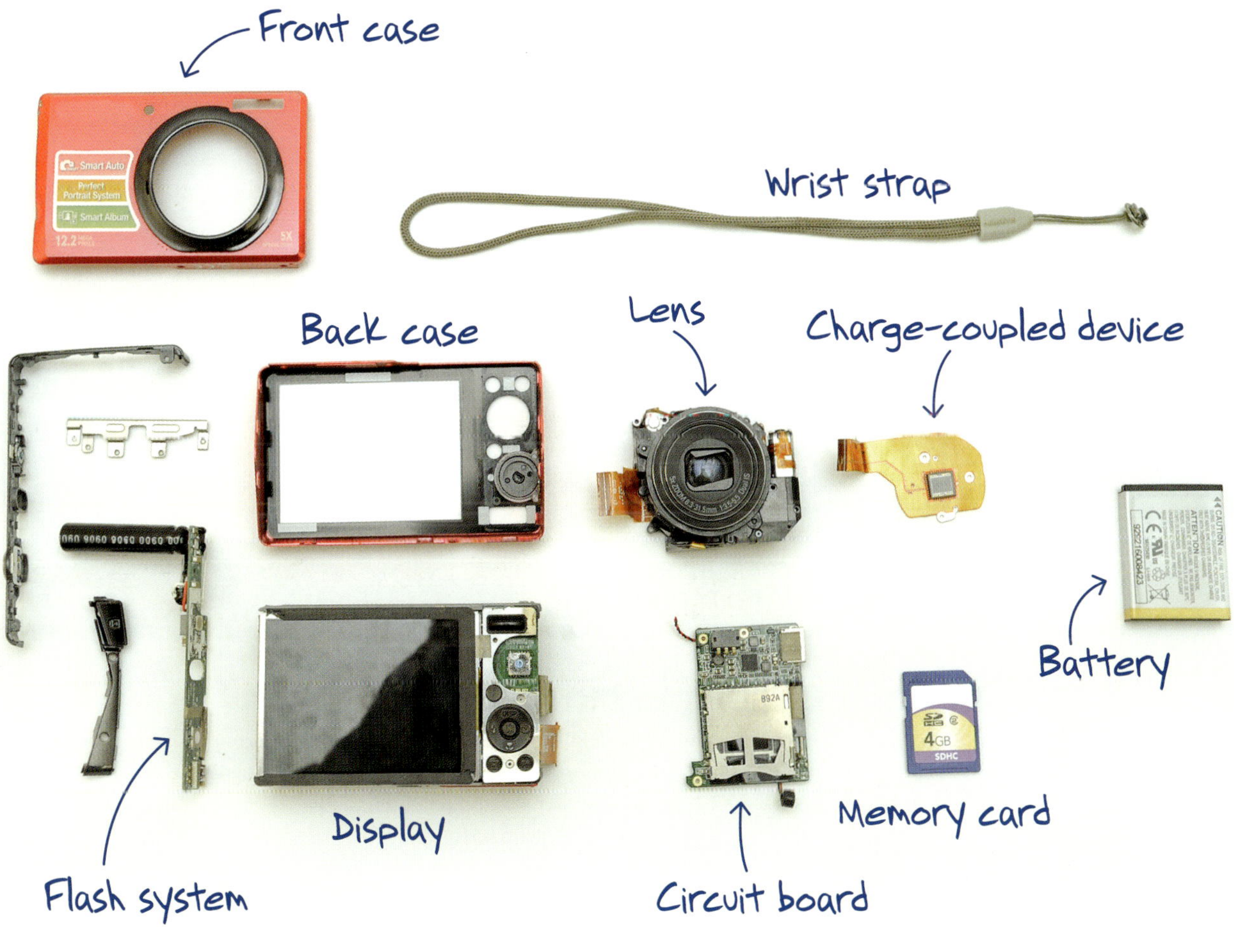
Front case
Wrist strap
Back case
Lens
Charge-coupled device
Battery
Flash system
Display
Circuit board
Memory card

Opening the Camera

Small screws hold the camera together. Remove all the screws you can see on the outside. Then you can pull the front off the camera. Inside you can see three major parts. They are the flash, the **lens**, and the **circuit board**.

Safety Note

The screwdriver is sharp, so be careful when removing the screws.

Safety Note

Pull out the battery before you start. Never try to open the battery.

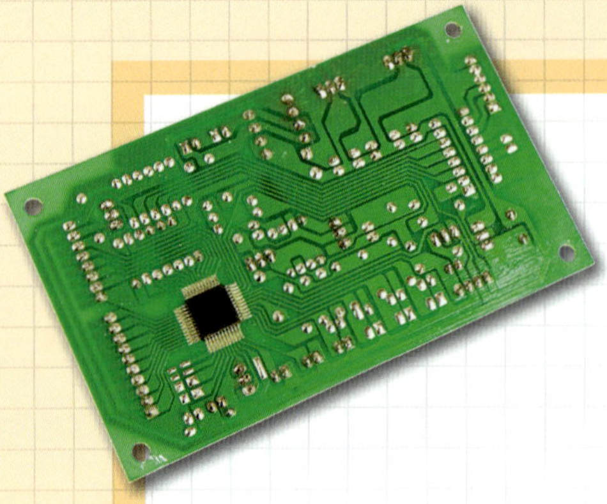

Flash

The flash system has a light and a **capacitor**. The capacitor stores up electricity. Then it releases the electricity to power the flash's light. The light can brighten up a dark scene. It lets people take photos in dim places.

Safety Note

The flash circuit board has sharp edges, so be careful when handling it.

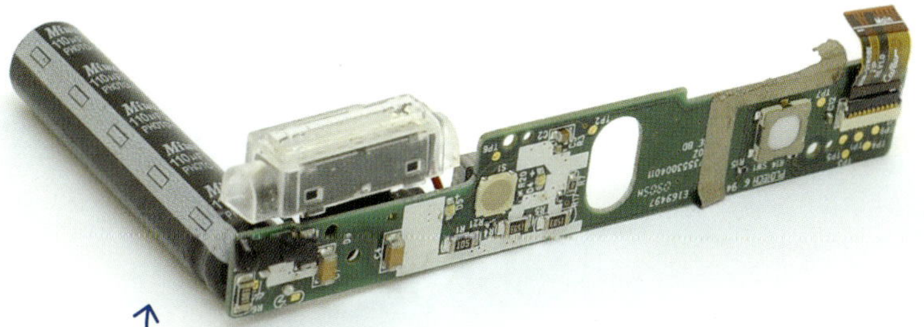

The capacitor is a black cylinder.

The capacitor and the flash connect to a small circuit board.

The Lens

Taking pictures is all about collecting light. The lens allows light to enter the camera. It is made up of pieces of glass. They are inside a plastic case. The pieces of glass move inside the lens. They shape how the light comes in. This lets the camera zoom in and out.

5x ZOOM 6.3-31.5mm 1:3.5-5.5 Dual IS
E1- ABICO

The Heart of the Camera

Small screws hold the lens in place. Remove them. Then pull the lens out. Behind the lens you can see the charge-coupled device (CCD). The CCD is what makes digital cameras possible. It collects light that comes in through the lens. Then it turns that light into an electrical **signal**.

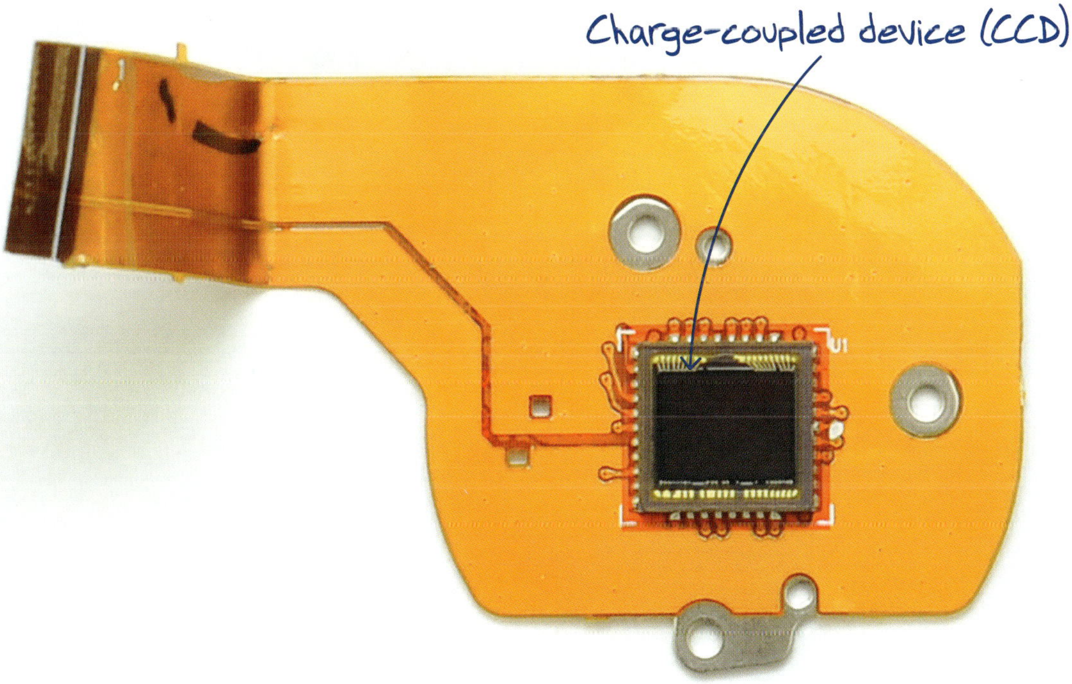
Charge-coupled device (CCD)
U1

The Circuit Board

Electrical signals from the CCD travel to the circuit board. There, **microchips** turn the signals into digital images.

The memory card fits into a slot on the circuit board.

Then the circuit board stores the images on a **memory card**. Users can plug the memory card into a computer to see the pictures.

The Display

The back of the camera has a large **display**. Users can see what the CCD is seeing when a picture is taken. They can also use the display to look at the images on the memory card. They can delete any images they don't want to keep.

0903 07-05
P/N:VG0373553007010
REV:1.0
DISP

Reusing a Digital Camera

We've taken apart a digital camera and learned what's inside. Now what? Here are some ideas for how to reuse the parts of a digital camera. Can you think of any more?

- **Mini Diorama**: With the insides taken out, the camera is an empty box with a big window for the lens. Can you craft a tiny scene inside the camera?
- **Going Smaller**: Think about the cameras in cell phones. What parts have to be made smaller? How might this affect the way cell phone cameras work?

Glossary

capacitor (kuh-PASS-uh-ter): A capacitor is an electronic part that stores electricity. A capacitor stores energy for the flash.

circuit board (SUR-kit BORD): A circuit board is a piece of material that holds computer chips, switches, and other parts. A circuit board is found inside the camera.

display (diss-PLAY): A display is a screen on electronic devices that shows information. The display shows what pictures have been taken.

lens (LENZ): A lens has pieces of curved glass that let light shine through. The lens shapes how light comes into the camera.

memory card (MEM-uh-ree KARD): A memory card is an object that can store digital information. The memory card stores digital images.

microchips (MY-kroh-chips): Microchips are parts that contain electrical circuits designed to do a certain job. In the camera, microchips turn electrical signals into digital images.

signal (SIG-nuhlz): A signal is an electrical pulse. A signal travels from the CCD to the circuit board.

To Learn More

IN THE LIBRARY

Holzweiss, Kristina. *Amazing Makerspace DIY with Electricity*. New York, NY: Scholastic, 2018.

Ives, Rob. *Fun Experiments with Light*. Minneapolis, MN: Hungry Tomato, 2018.

Nagelhout, Ryan. *The Problem with Early Cameras*. New York, NY: Gareth Stevens, 2016.

ON THE WEB

Visit our website for links about taking apart a digital camera: **childsworld.com/links**

Note to Parents, Teachers, and Librarians: We routinely verify our Web links to make sure they are safe and active sites. So encourage your readers to check them out!

Index

Smart Auto
Perfect Portrait System
Smart Album
12.2 MEGA PIXELS
5X